W9-BSY-385

To Alan Charles Proctor

ILLUSTRATIONS: Scarlet macaws *above and front cover*;
red-and-green macaws and scarlet macaws *back cover*;
heliconius butterfly, fiery topaz hummingbirds, and egret
front endpapers; egrets, spectacled owls, and jaguar *back endpapers*.

PRONUNCIATION GUIDE: The names of animals and plants are
pronounced as they are spelled with the exception of Hoatzin, which
is pronounced oo-at-zin.

KINGFISHER BOOKS
Grisewood & Dempsey Inc.
95 Madison Avenue
New York, New York 10016

First American edition 1993

2 4 6 8 10 9 7 5 3 1

Text copyright © Tanis Jordan 1993
Illustrations copyright © Martin Jordan 1993

All rights reserved under International and Pan-American
Copyright Conventions.

Library of Congress Cataloging-in-Publication Data
Jordan, Martin
Jungle days, jungle nights / Martin and Tanis Jordan. — 1st
American ed.
p.   cm.
Summary: Describes some of the mammals, reptiles, and
insects that live, both day and night, in the jungles of South
America.
1. Jungle fauna—South America—Juvenile literature. 2.
Jungle ecology—South America—Juvenile literature. [1. Jungle
animals. 2. Jungle ecology.] I. Jordan, Tanis   II. Title.
QL235.J67   1993
574.5'2642—dc 20   92–40366   CIP   AC

ISBN 1–85697–885–0

Designed by Caroline Johnson
Printed in Hong Kong

JUNGLE DAYS JUNGLE NIGHTS

Martin and Tanis Jordan

Kingfisher Books

NEW YORK

Juv. QL 235.J67 1993

In a green steaming jungle in South America is a swirling, gurgling river. The water is cloudy and colored khaki by the mud washed from the riverbanks. On a sandbank grows a stilt-rooted tree, and hidden among its roots is the nest of a spectacled caiman.

In the rainy season it rains every day and nearly every night. But now the dry season is just beginning. Each day it will rain less than the day before until it hardly rains at all.

Just after dawn, as a milky white mist drifts up from the river, a sound comes from inside the nest—"Peep, peep, peep." A big knobbly brown head bursts out of the water. Sixty-six snapping teeth glint in the sun. The spectacled caiman listens.

"Peep, peep, peep." From inside the eggs, the baby caimans are calling their mother. Most of the hatchlings have broken out of the eggs, using a special hatching tooth on the ends of their snouts, but some are still struggling. Picking up the unbroken eggs in her jaws, the caiman gently cracks the shells with her tongue. When they are all hatched, she leads her young into the river.

At the end of the sandbank, a narrow creek flows into the river. Shaded by giant trees, it is like a leafy tunnel. The water is clear, and stained the color of cola by falling leaves. In the dappled sunlight a giant otter surfaces among the water lily pads. Snorting to his mate on the bank, he plunges under the water. He closes his nose and ears but keeps his eyes wide open as he chases a fish.

In the afternoons, when everything is quiet, the otters begin digging into the riverbank with their webbed feet. Humming to each other as they work, they dig a tunnel leading into a den. Usually the giant otters sleep curled up on the riverbank, but now that the dry season is here and their cubs are due, they must prepare a safe, dry place in which the cubs can be born.

At the other end of the winding creek is a shimmering lake. In a tree, overhanging the water, two downy hoatzin chicks have climbed out of their nest to explore. Their parents are in a lily bush not far away, swallowing leaves to bring back to their chicks.

Slithering up the tree is an emerald tree snake. She flicks out her tongue, tasting the air for the scent of baby birds. Stealthily the glittering green snake coils her tail around a branch, but just as she is about to strike, the chicks see her and hurl themselves straight down into the lake below. They hide among the water plants until, with a hiss, the snake glides away. Then, using the two special claws on their wings, the chicks clamber up to the nest. When their parents return they are hanging up to dry.

From the other side of the lake comes a great commotion. Whooping and shrieking, a troop of smoky woolly monkeys is foraging for food. As the monkeys bound acrobatically through the trees, a young one dawdles behind. Chattering crossly, his mother calls to him to stay with the troop. She knows that huge harpy eagles and sharp-shinned hawks are always eager to pluck a lone monkey from the trees with their sharp talons.

High in the topmost branches the young monkey finds a bromeliad, a plant like the top of an enormous pineapple. Among its leaves are pools of water. But as he reaches up for a drink a frog hops out. The monkey springs back in surprise. It is a poison arrow frog. The frog is only one inch long, but her brilliant colors are a warning that she is very poisonous.

She had laid her eggs on the ground and guarded them until that morning, when they hatched into tadpoles. Quickly she helped them to wriggle onto her back, two at a time, then set off up a tree to find a bromeliad. Stepping onto a leaf, she leaned back so the tadpoles could drop into the water. She hopped up and down the tree until all the tadpoles were safe. Each day she must climb up and feed them until they grow into frogs.

Now it hasn't rained very much for weeks. The dry season is at its driest. The trees are fruiting and food is abundant. As the sun sinks and the forest floor becomes dark and gloomy, a pair of spotted pacas peer out from among the giant tree roots. Whiskers twitching, they trot daintily through the forest, snuffling around until they find figs that have fallen from a tree. Pacas are vegetarians, and their favorite food is ripe fruit.

As the pacas nibble the fruit, another creature creeps closer, a young ocelot. Ocelots are carnivorous, and their favorite food is meat. But the ocelot is still learning how to stalk prey, and she rustles the leaves. The pacas have exceptional ears and nervous noses. For an instant they freeze: not a whisker quivers, not a toenail trembles. Then, in a flurry of flying feet they flee.

By the end of the dry season there is hardly any rain. Purple jacaranda trees blaze with blossoms. Beside the stilt-rooted tree, the river has dwindled to a shallow stream. The sandbank is high and wide, and from rocks on the riverbed birds watch for fish.

Late one sizzlingly hot afternoon, two fiery topaz hummingbirds hover on humming wings beside a passion flower vine to dip their bills into the blossoms. Because they use so much energy to fly, hummingbirds need to drink nectar from more than a thousand flowers every day.

A heliconius butterfly flutters by and settles on a leaf. Passion flower leaves contain a poison. But when this butterfly was a caterpillar it fed on the glossy leaves and absorbed the poison. Birds and lizards won't eat it because it tastes horrible.

One hot sticky night when the jungle is wilting from lack of rain, a tropical screech owl leaves his nest in a hole in a mahogany tree to swoop through the jungle on silent wings. His big round eyes make use of the moonlight as he searches for food to carry back to his owlets. The owl settles on a branch and listens. His keen ears hear the faint sound of a mouse cleaning its whiskers. His powerful eyes catch the slight movement of a beetle walking up a branch on a distant tree.

Far away, beyond the hills, fingers of lightning fork through the sky. Thunder grumbles and drums in the distance. The owl watches the storm light the jungle an eerie green. And then comes a wind fierce enough to puff the pacas off their feet, to blow the owl from his perch, and to whirl the woolly monkeys from the trees.

As the owl flies home, a great drumming noise comes closer and louder until it fills the jungle. The rain is coming. Now it will rain every day and nearly every night. Rivers will swell and burst their banks, and the jungle will be flooded. All this the owl knows because it happens every year.

At first only a few drops of rain drip through the thick, tangled ceiling of leaves. But gradually the rain pours through everywhere. It fills the bromeliads to overflowing. It streams down the branches and runs in rivulets down millions of leaves, making great puddles on the ground.

That night there is a tremendous explosion. A tree is struck by lightning and catches fire. The tree is three hundred years old, and the ancient wood burns so fiercely that even the rain cannot put out the flames. Creatures scatter. Two jaguars escape just in time as, with a great groan, the tree falls.

Now it rains so heavily that the puddles join up and stream down into the creek. The creek flows faster with all the extra water and gushes out into the river. The river is rising fast. Massive tree trunks are swept along and tossed around like pencils.

And at last, the water that ran down the owl's tree, that poured on the pacas, that washed over the woolly monkeys, begins its journey to the world's biggest river, the Amazon, to flow three thousand miles to the Atlantic Ocean.

The rain stops. The jungle drips. Now sunlight filters through to the jungle floor. Curious creatures come closer to investigate. A basilisk lizard wriggles out from under a palm frond, his orange eyes gazing around for inattentive insects to eat.

With nostrils quivering, a brown brocket deer nibbles fern fronds. She moves toward the edge of the clearing, licking her nose to test the way of the wind. She stops abruptly, sniffs the air, and barks in alarm. Smoke! Even after all that rain, the fire is still glowing. She raises her tail, showing the white hair underneath, to alert other deer. Her big ears swivel as she listens for sounds of danger.

Suddenly, the fire pops and spits out sparks. The deer skitters away. Startled, the basilisk lizard rises up onto his hind legs, raises his tail for balance, and streaks through the jungle, down to the creek and across the surface of the water without sinking.

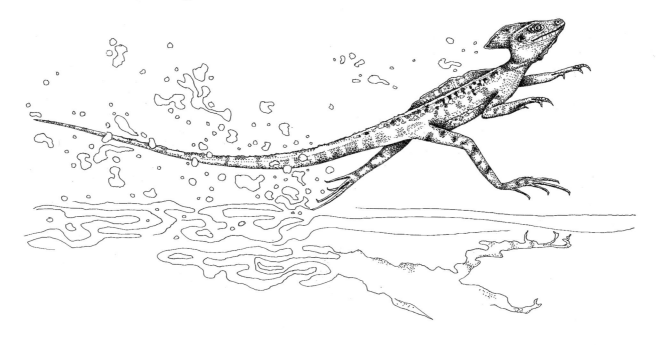

As the weeks go by the skies are gray and heavy with clouds. The jungle is damp and clammy. Now it rains every day and there are thunderstorms most nights. By the middle of the rainy season three feet of rain has fallen.

In a silk cotton tree, nearly 200 feet tall, are two harpy eagles, the mightiest eagles in the world. From their perch, they survey the crowns of thousands and thousands of trees. And in every single tree something is happening, from a prowling jaguar padding along a bough, to tiny termites devouring dead twigs. In the distance a flaming coral tree sheds its last blooms, and from the hard wood of a mahogany tree comes the *boi-ng-ng-ng* of a woodpecker.

When the rainy season is at its rainiest the river rises fifteen feet. Now the sandbank is submerged, and the river has flooded into the forest. Even part of the stilt-rooted tree is under the water.

The giant otters and their cubs have vanished into the jungle. The hoatzin chicks are growing, and the special claws on their wings drop off.

The caimans are growing too, and have lost the hatching tooth on the end of their snouts. All the young creatures born in the dry season are learning how to live in the jungle.

Late one hot and humid afternoon, the caimans wriggle into the river to cool down. As they glide toward the stilt-rooted tree an enormous creature looms out of the deep water. It is an Orinoco crocodile, twenty feet long and over seventy years old. During her life she has swallowed stones from the riverbed to make her heavier and help her stay hidden under the water. But reptiles can't breathe under water, so she has come up for air.

The Orinoco crocodile prefers to eat fish, but now, because the rivers are so deep, fish are hard to find and she will eat anything, even spectacled caimans. Frantically the young caimans swim toward their mother who hustles them to hide among the flooded forest trees.

One evening at sunset, as storm clouds mass in the western sky, a band of capybaras gather on the shore. Like giant guinea pigs, they jostle nervously against each other. Capybaras are the world's largest rodents and superb swimmers, but at dawn and dusk they are wary of swimming because this is the time when the largest snake in the world, the anaconda, waits in the lake for its prey.

Toward the end of the rainy season less and less rain falls. The skies are blue for most of the day, and the sunsets are pink and orange again. Now, with just an occasional thunder shower to remember it by, the rainy season ends.

In the bright moonlight a tiny mouse opossum climbs out of a hollow cocoa pod and briskly begins to clean her silky coat. Marching down the cocoa tree is a procession of busy brown leafcutter ants. Along the branches, down the trunk, and over the ground they go, each ant carrying in its jaws a piece of shiny leaf.

As they march along, speck-sized flies hover above them, eager to lay their eggs on the ants' necks. If they succeed, the eggs will hatch and maggots will eat the ants' brains. But riding on each piece of leaf are small worker ants and, as the flies swoop down, the worker ants stab at them with their sharp pincers to keep them away.

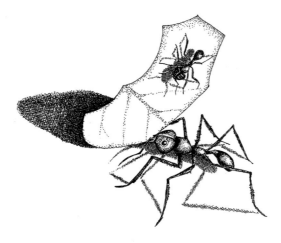

The ants are hurrying to their vast underground nest where worker ants chew the leaves into a mush. On the mush they grow a garden of fungus. The fungus is the only food the ants can eat, and the ants' nest is the only place in the world where this fungus can grow.

On certain nights when the moon is round and full and there are no clouds in the sky, a male night monkey comes out and calls:

"Hoot hoot, hoot hoot."

He is warning other night monkeys not to step inside his territory to eat from his food trees.

Soon the branches and leaves of a strangler fig begin rustling and shaking as his family, a female and two young monkeys, join him on the end of the branch. While all the other monkeys in the world sleep at night, night monkeys are out from dusk until dawn, and they sleep in the daytime. The night monkey's hoots echo across the river, where, in a trail of reflected moonlight, shine the eyes of a young spectacled caiman.

In a gum tree two pygmy marmosets, the smallest monkeys in the world, are squabbling over a fruit. With a formidable squawk, a blue-headed parrot skids onto the branch near them. The parrot wants to crack the stone inside the fruit with his powerful beak and eat the soft kernel. He lunges at the marmosets, pretending to be fierce. They crouch together, twittering at the bird, pretending to be brave. But the marmosets will not be bullied. They realize that they have nothing to fear from the parrot.

On the jungle floor, forest flies dart around a white stinkhorn fungus, enticed by its pungent perfume. Hanging from a twig, a female katydid is listening for the brrrr-ip, brrrr-ip call of a male katydid. She looks like a leaf, and so she depends on the trees to hide her.

Like the katydid, everything in the jungle depends on the trees, because without them there would be no nooks for nests, no cool cola-colored creeks for otters, no security for snakes, and nowhere to tip tadpoles. Without the trees there would be no fruit to feed on, no cocoa pods to sleep in, and no nips of nectar.

As the sun comes up and the milky white mist drifts away, a young caiman leaves the river to bask in the morning sunshine. She stays so still, steaming in the sun, that clouds of phoebis butterflies settle around her to feed. The caiman is one year old today.